-completely unscrupulous books-
by Liesl-Yvette

A Balloon and a Bear
Around the Corner & on the Left
Fair Horribolous
Evil-or a Plan for World Domination

All titles published by:
Tullulah and Bear Publications UK
38 Balham High Rd London SW12 9AH

love unrequited

by Liesl-Yvette Wilson

A Completely Unscrupulous Book
Published by Tullulah & Bear
London United Kingdom

2008 by Liesl-Yvette Wilson
All rights reserved

ISBN: 987-0-9550752-2-6

No part of this book may be reproduced,
stored in retrieval system, or transmitted by any
means, electronic, mechanical, photocopying,
recording, or otherwise without written
permission.

For Sparrow

love?

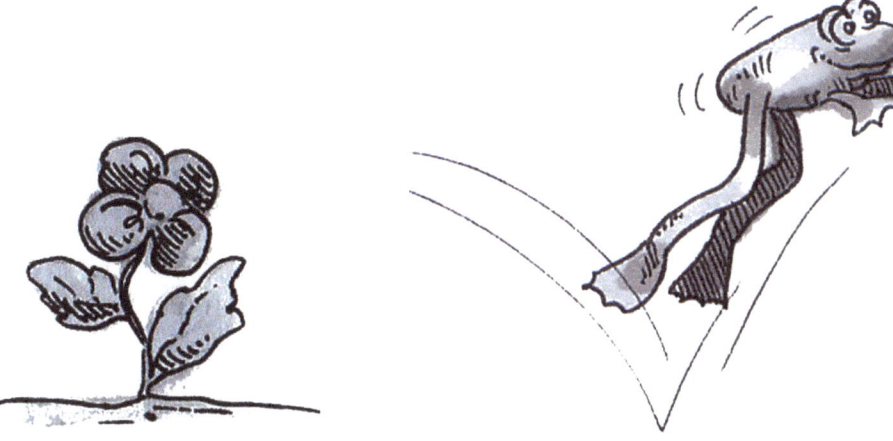

Sugar and Spice...

You can contact Tullulah - just email;
tullulahsbear@googlemail.com

www.ingramcontent.com/pod-product-compliance
Lightning Source LLC
Chambersburg PA
CBHW042014150426
43196CB00002B/46

9 780955 975226